JUNIATA COLLEGE LIBRARY

P9-CEP-611

DO NOT REMOVE
THIS BOOK FROM
THE LIBRARY

LEGENDS
OF THE WEST

The Black Cowboys

Butch Cassidy

Wyatt Earp

The Gunslingers

Jesse James

Annie Oakley

LEGENDS OF THE WEST

JESSE JAMES

John Wukovits

CHELSEA HOUSE PUBLISHERS
Philadelphia

Chelsea House Publishers

Editorial Director Richard Rennert
Production Manager Pamela Loos
Art Director Sara Davis
Picture Editor Judy Hasday

Staff for **JESSE JAMES**

Senior Editor John Ziff
Editorial Assistant Kristine Brennan
Designer Alison Burnside
Picture Researcher Sandy Jones
Cover Design and Digital Illustration Alison Burnside

Copyright © 1997 by Chelsea House Publishers, a division of Main Line Book Co.
All rights reserved. Printed and bound in the United States of America.

3 5 7 9 8 6 4 2

Library of Congress Cataloging-in-Publication Data

Wukovits, John F., 1944-
    Jesse James/John Wukovits
        p. cm. — (Legends of the West)
    Includes bibliographical references (p.) and index.
    Summary: Discusses the life of Jesse James, from his beginnings as a teenage guerilla soldier for the Confederates, through his career as a robber with the James-Younger gang, to his murder at the hands of a former gang member.
    ISBN 0-7910-3876-9
    1. James, Jesse, 1847-1882—Juvenile literature. 2. Outlaws—West (U.S.)—Biography—Juvenile literature. 3. Frontier and pioneer life—West (U.S.)—Juvenile literature. 4. West (U.S.)—Biography—Juvenile literature. [1. James, Jesse, 1847-1882. 2. Robbers and outlaws. 3. Frontier and pioneer life—West (U.S.) 4. West (U.S.)—History.] I. Title. II. Series.
F594.J27W84 1996   96-38468
364.1' 552'092—dc20   CIP
[B]   AC

Curr
F
594
.J27
W84
1996

CONTENTS

─── ★ ───

9-1-98 Chelsea House (Elvenshade Endow) Jm 12.76

MURDER AT NOON

As high noon drew near on December 7, 1869, a lull descended on the small western town of Gallatin, Missouri. Most of the peaceful community's citizens had taken a break from their work to eat lunch. Inside the Daviess County Savings Bank, cashier John W. Sheets and clerk William A. McDowell quietly went about their jobs as usual.

A slight noise at the door attracted Sheets's attention. A stranger walked in, casually strolled up to the counter, and asked the cashier if he could have change for a $100 bill. This request was not out of the ordinary, so Sheets obliged the respectable-looking man without hesitation.

An engraving depicting Jesse James's cold-blooded murder of John Sheets, a cashier at the Daviess County Savings Bank in Gallatin, Missouri. Jesse blamed Sheets, a former Union captain, for the death of his Confederate commander, William "Bloody Bill" Anderson. The artist's assumption that Jesse and Frank James wore masks during the crime is erroneous; before the Gallatin job the brothers were unknown to the law.

As Sheets counted out the change, another nice-looking man—a broad-shouldered, sandy-haired young fellow with bright blue eyes and a turned-up nose—stepped inside the door and whispered something to the first man. Suddenly, before the unsuspecting cashier knew what hit him, the second stranger whipped out a Colt Navy pistol and cold-bloodedly shot Sheets twice, in the head and chest. His lifeless body crumpled to the floor. Horrified, McDowell dashed for the door, but before he reached safety, a bullet from the Colt pistol pierced his arm. The bank clerk staggered outside and sounded the alarm.

Realizing they had little time to escape before the townspeople reacted, the two robbers ran behind the counter and hurriedly stuffed about $700 into a sack. Bullets whizzed by as they sprinted into the street. The first robber skillfully hopped onto his horse and started to gallop away, but the second ran into trouble. Just as the man tried to mount, his frightened horse bolted, tangling the robber's foot in the stirrup. The horse dragged the outlaw several feet down Gallatin's main avenue before he could free himself. His partner sped back, pulled the mountless thief onto his own horse, and raced out of town.

Riding two to a horse through unfamiliar terrain, the criminals would not be able to evade the sheriff's posse for long. A mile out of town, however, they stole a horse from a local farmer who had the bad luck to ride by. Then they kidnapped a minister and forced him to guide them through the area's desolate back roads, vanishing with their loot.

Seeking to bring the duo to justice for the ruthless crime, Gallatin authorities interviewed the eyewitnesses and gathered clues. The gunman's abandoned horse, an exceptionally fine specimen, proved useful in identifying the bandit. On December 16 the *Kansas City Times* printed a story that traced the horse back to Jesse James, "whose mother and stepfather live about four miles from Centreville [the old name for the town of Kearney, in Clay County, Missouri]. Both he and his brother are desperate men, having had much experience in horse and revolver work."

The authorities' suspicions were heightened when they discovered that Jesse James had a strong motive for Sheets's murder. Both the bank clerk, William McDowell, and the minister who had been kidnapped remembered that the gunman had accused Sheets and a man named Cox of being responsible for the death of his brother. Acting on this tip, investigators found that Sheets had fought as a Union captain under Major S. P. Cox in the Civil War battle that claimed the life of Confederate guerrilla commander William "Bloody Bill" Anderson. Jesse had publicly sworn to avenge the death of Anderson, the leader he fondly considered his brother.

On the strength of this evidence, Gallatin businessmen posted a generous $3,000 reward for the capture of Jesse James and his brother, Frank. Missouri governor Joseph McClurg, expressing outrage at the crime, ordered the local militia to catch the murderous thieves. Daviess County deputy sheriff John Thomason and three of his men rode out to the James family farm in Clay County to arrest the suspects. Just as they arrived at the house, though, the James brothers—who had been warned of the raid by friendly locals—burst out of the barn on horseback. They spurred their horses to jump

The trail of clues in the murder of John Sheets led authorities to the Kearney, Missouri, farm of Zerelda and Reuben Samuel, the James brothers' mother and step-father. This photograph shows the farm's original house, in which Frank and Jesse James were born.

the barnyard fence, and when Thomason followed and caught up with them, Jesse calmly shot the lawman's horse out from under him.

For the next year, the James brothers remained beyond the law's reach, protected by loyal relatives, friends, and neighbors. Family members, though they knew otherwise, swore that Jesse had been at home on the day of the crime and that his horse had been sold to someone from Kansas two days before the robbery. Despite the solid case against him, his allies successfully shielded him from justice.

All things considered, the James brothers' first big solo crime—they had participated in other gangs for several years before leading their own—had been extremely successful. Their thrilling escape had already made them famous, and Jesse took advantage of the press to further aid his case. *Kansas City Times* newspaperman John Newman Edwards, a former Confederate major who had befriended the brothers during the Civil War, published statements from "upright" citizens asserting that the accused criminals were honest, decent men. The paper also printed a letter from Jesse (which was most likely written by Edwards) in which he claimed he was an innocent, "peaceable citizen" but would never receive a fair trial as a Confederate veteran.

Through a combination of clever publicity, deceit, misplaced allegiance, luck, and sheer boldness, Jesse had frustrated the law and captured the public's imagination. His legendary career of robbery, murder, and mayhem had begun.

STORMY BEGINNINGS

The man who would become one of the nation's most notorious outlaws was born into a tightly knit, religious family. Jesse's parents met while his mother, Zerelda Cole, was attending a Catholic convent school in Lexington, Kentucky, and his father, Robert James, was studying at a nearby seminary. After Robert was ordained a Baptist minister in 1841, the young couple married and went to visit family in northwestern Missouri. The newlyweds chose to settle near the small town of Kearney in Clay County after the idealistic Robert observed that the region—a wild, sometimes violent area on the border of Indian lands—could use some good preachers. It was a fateful decision. The rough-and-tumble atmosphere of the part of Missouri called the Border would shape the Jameses' sons even more than would the family's religious beliefs.

Jesse James, age 17, already a fearsome guerrilla fighter. Note the guns tucked into his belt—he carried as many as six pistols at a time and could shoot accurately with both hands while holding the reins of a galloping horse between his teeth.

The couple prospered in the frontier town, where they joined a community of other transplanted Southerners. Through hard work, they expanded their farm to 275 acres and raised sheep, cattle, and horses in addition to food crops. Their family grew as well: son Alexander Franklin (nicknamed Frank) was born on January 10, 1843. A second son, Robert, died in infancy, but a healthy baby whom they named Jesse Woodson was born on September 5, 1847, followed by Susan Lavenia on November 25, 1849.

Robert James spent a great deal of time away from the family farm, attending to his preaching duties. An enthusiastic, energetic minister, he not only expanded his congregation at the New Hope Baptist Church but also founded two other churches. In between traveling to revival meetings, he helped found the Liberty Baptist Association and nearby William Jewell College as well.

While her husband was away, the tasks of maintaining the farm and raising the children fell to Zerelda, a capable, strong-minded woman who was fiercely protective of her offspring. The close bonds between mother and children intensified in 1850 when Robert James joined a party of gold miners, intending to spend a year on the West Coast establishing more Baptist churches. Within three weeks of arriving in California, the zealous minister fell ill with pneumonia and died.

Seeking support for the family, Zerelda soon remarried. However, she quickly left her second husband, Benjamin Simms, because she felt he mistreated Frank and Jesse. In 1855, when Jesse was eight, she found a more appropriate stepfather in Reuben Samuel. A mild-mannered,

The homestead where Jesse and Frank James grew up. Situated on a 275-acre farm in Clay County, Missouri, it provided the brothers with a refuge throughout much of their career in crime. Family members and Clay County friends and neighbors could always be counted on to shield the pair from the law.

reliable doctor, Samuel liked the boys and did not interfere in how Zerelda raised them. The happy couple had four children together: Archie, John, Sallie, and Fannie.

The family led an ordinary life as upstanding citizens of Clay County. Jesse and Frank went to Pleasant Grove School but spent most of their time working on the farm, where they learned to ride horses and handle firearms. Each week they attended church with the family, and Jesse exhibited his father's strong religious faith. (In fact, throughout his later life of crime, he remained a devout churchgoer.) Frank inherited their father's love of learning and used his spare time to read; according to legend, he liked to quote Shakespeare.

Although farm life was fairly quiet, Zerelda Samuel had good reason to be protective of her children. Violence and sudden death were commonplace throughout the Border, where Indians, outlaws, or extreme weather could snuff out a life in an instant. To make matters worse, in the 1850s settlers clashed bitterly over slavery. Northerners poured into neighboring Kansas, aiming to make it a free state, which

There is no disputing that guerrilla commander William "Bloody Bill" Anderson earned his nickname. He refused to take prisoners, and his men frequently scalped or mutilated their victims. Anderson considered Jesse James his "keenest and cleanest fighter."

angered Southern slaveholders. Bands of pro-slavery Missourians regularly crossed into Kansas to attack abolitionists (people who wanted to end slavery) and to illegally vote in the territory's elections. And antislavery Kansans fought back.

When the Civil War broke out in 1861, the James family—which owned seven slaves—passionately supported the Confederacy, although Missouri remained under Union control. Eighteen-year-old Frank James rushed to fight for the South, and by 1863 he was ambushing Federal troops, cutting telegraph lines, and burning bridges with William Clarke Quantrill's bushwhackers, a ferocious force of guerrilla soldiers. (Guerrillas are fighters whose units are independent of the regular army. Their tactics—including quick, surprise attacks and sabotage—are designed to harass and disrupt the enemy army.) At 15, Jesse was too young to fight, but he and his mother acted as lookouts for the bushwhackers.

Because of their Confederate ties, the James-Samuel family was harassed by Federal troops. One June day in 1863, a group rode onto the Samuel farm and tried to bully Zerelda, who was pregnant at the time, into giving them information about the guerrillas. They strung a rope around Dr. Samuel's neck, threw one end of the rope over a tree branch, and hauled him up until his feet were off the ground. After letting him down before he suffocated, they pulled him up again. Although they repeated this painful torment several times, the soldiers got no information from Zerelda or her husband, and they eventually gave up. Before they left the farm, though, they whipped Jesse for his Southern sympathies.

Jesse greatly desired revenge, and his resolve deepened a few months later when the state militia arrested his mother and sister on suspicion of helping the Confederate forces. In the spring of 1864, he was finally allowed to join the guerrillas, becoming part of a fierce unit led by one of Quantrill's lieutenants, Bloody Bill Anderson. Following a "take no prisoners" policy, Anderson's men were notorious for their savagery, often scalping their Union victims (slicing off the skin and hair from the tops of the men's heads).

Though only 16 years old, Jesse proved himself to be as capable—and bloodthirsty—in battle as any of his fellow guerrillas. With his eagerness to fight and his quick sense of humor, the teenager was popular with the older bushwhackers. They teasingly nicknamed him "Dingus," after the odd curse he had shouted when he accidentally shot off the tip of his left-hand middle finger. (Years later, as a robber, Jesse always wore gloves to keep from being identified.)

Jesse showed himself to be a quick learner of valuable guerrilla skills, such as scouting locations for good hiding spots. In no time, he was able to control a galloping horse using only his teeth to hold the reins, leaving both hands free to fire revolvers. He learned to wear as many as six guns so he would not have to reload as often, and he practiced until he could shoot accurately without wasting time on aiming. In fact, Jesse demonstrated such talent that Anderson declared him "the keenest and cleanest fighter in the command."

Jesse, like the other members of his unit, saw and did his share of cold-blooded killing. In September 1864, only a month after suffering a near-fatal chest wound, he rejoined Anderson's band and participated in a massacre of Union soldiers at Centralia, Missouri. The guerrillas seized and looted the town, burned its railroad station, and placed railroad ties across the tracks to stop the noon train from the east. Among the train's passengers were 35 Union soldiers, unarmed because they were traveling home on leave. The bushwhackers stripped the soldiers of their uniforms (which were saved for disguises) and proceeded to gun them down. After mutilating the soldiers' dead bodies, Anderson's men set fire to the train and sent it racing out of control down the tracks before abandoning Centralia.

Soon a Union force commanded by Major A. V. E. Johnson thundered toward the guerrillas' camp to exact vengeance for the Centralia massacre. As Johnson's troops approached, the bushwhackers deployed in a line facing them. When the guerrillas dismounted, the Union commander concluded that they were going to fight on foot and ordered his men to dismount as well. After every fourth soldier had led all the Union horses off the field, the guerrillas quickly remounted their own horses and galloped toward the enemy, wildly whooping and shooting. Jesse led the charge, killing Major Johnson and some of the other 124 Union soldiers who perished, many of whom were chased down and shot from behind as they ran in all directions.

By this time, though, the tide of the Civil War had turned in the Union's favor. After taking part in a failed mission to assassinate President Abraham Lincoln, Frank James reluctantly surrendered to Union troops in July 1865. Jesse had escaped to Texas but returned to Missouri in June 1865 because many Southern soldiers who had surrendered had been allowed to go home. However, the bushwhackers were so hated for their brutality that when Union forces saw a group of guerrillas riding toward Lexington, Missouri, under a white flag of surrender, the Federal soldiers opened fire. Jesse was once again badly wounded in the chest and barely managed to crawl to safety. After a night in the woods, he was found by a farmer, who took the teenager to his house.

On the brink of death, Jesse somehow traveled to Rulo, Nebraska, where his family had been forced to resettle. He begged his mother to take him back to Missouri so he would not die in a Northern state. She granted his wish and brought him to Harlem, Missouri, where her sister-in-law, Mrs. John Mimms, ran a boardinghouse. Amazingly, Jesse's teenage cousin, Zerelda Mimms (who was named after his mother), nursed him back to health. The two fell in love and agreed that they would eventually get married.

By the end of that summer, the whole family was reunited. While Jesse recovered, Dr. Samuel and Frank began rebuilding their Clay County farm, which had been devastated by the war. Each Sunday Jesse attended the local Baptist church, where he sang in the choir and was baptized.

At not quite 18 years of age, Jesse James had already survived two near-fatal chest wounds, developed into a seasoned killer, and become engaged to be married. But the idea of settling down to a quiet life on the farm did not appeal to him. He was ready to employ his deadly skills in a promising new career—crime.

Zerelda Samuel, the fierce, devoted mother of Frank and Jesse James.

3

THE MAKING
OF A LEGEND

Jesse James claimed that he turned to crime because he was treated unfairly by Northerners during and after the Civil War. In the post–Civil War period known as Reconstruction, the Radical Republicans (a rabidly anti-South branch of Lincoln's party) who controlled Missouri *did* discriminate against Southern veterans. Anyone who refused to take an oath swearing that he had done nothing disloyal to the Union—including mere verbal support of the Confederacy—had trouble finding a job. However, most Confederates survived the hard times without becoming outlaws. Most likely, Jesse chose a life of crime because he saw how easy it was to rob banks. In the wild, lawless Border area, an outlaw who knew the woods and back roads could readily escape on horse-

Jesse James (left) poses with members of his gang in this photograph from the 1870s. He thoroughly enjoyed the excitement and notoriety that came with being an outlaw bandit.

back—and have more money and excitement than a farmer or preacher ever would.

In 1866 some of Jesse's bushwhacker friends and relatives—Frank James was probably among them—decided to attempt their first bank robbery in broad daylight. They successfully robbed the Clay County Savings Bank in Liberty, Missouri, riding away with more than $60,000. Realizing that he could use his shooting and riding skills to steal a lot of money, Jesse joined up with the gang of ex-guerrillas as soon as his chest wound was fully healed.

One of his earliest jobs occurred on March 2, 1867. Jesse and five other gang members rode into Savannah, Missouri, around noon and strolled into the bank. Suspicious, the banker rushed to shut the safe door. When he refused to reopen the vault, the bandits shot him, left him for dead (he later recovered), and fled the town empty-handed.

Several months later the outlaws pulled a more profitable—and more deadly—heist in Richmond, Missouri. The gang, which included the James brothers and some of the Younger brothers—who would later play a major role in Jesse James's criminal exploits—split up into small groups and took different routes to the Hughes and Mason Bank. About eight gang members waited outside while four others entered the bank with guns drawn and seized $4,000.

Richmond's citizens resisted the robbery, opening fire as the bandits burst out of the bank. Jesse and the gang wheeled their horses around and charged the townspeople ferociously, gunning down Mayor John Shaw as well as a father and son. Speeding out of town, the outlaws split up to confuse the posse. The outraged towns-

In February 1866 a gang of Jesse's relatives and Confederate comrades—probably including Frank James—robbed the Clay County Savings Bank in Liberty, Missouri. The ease of the robbery, combined with the $60,000 haul, encouraged Jesse to join the gang as soon as a wartime chest wound had healed.

people took revenge by lynching several suspected gang members over the next few months.

In search of a less dangerous area to rob, the gang turned to Kentucky. Cole Younger, one of the James brothers' former Confederate commanders, posed as a cattle buyer to scout the Nimrod Long Bank in Russellville. In March 1868 the gang stole more than $12,000 from the bank, but the owner hired a private detective to catch the thieves. Because of his efforts, several of the outlaws were killed or imprisoned.

The James brothers were luckier. Although the detective suspected their participation, he was unable to connect them to the crime. In fact, unlike the roughly 30 outlaws he worked with over the years, Jesse seemed to lead a charmed life, continually emerging from tight scrapes unharmed.

With most of its original members either captured or killed, the band that had robbed the Clay County Savings Bank in 1866 became the James-Younger gang, headed by the James brothers and Cole Younger. Fearless and cunning, Jesse would eventually become the group's

For nearly a decade, the Younger brothers formed a vital part of the James gang. Pictured here are (from left) Bob, Jim, and Cole, along with their sister. Another brother, John, was killed by a Pinkerton agent.

undisputed leader. For the moment, though, he and the other gang members decided to lie low to avoid capture. Jesse may even have taken a steamship to California and spent time as a cowboy on his uncle's Paso Robles ranch. But when their money began to run out, the James brothers struck again—this time in Gallatin, Missouri. The 1869 murder of bank cashier John Sheets and the brothers' spectacular escape from the law attracted public attention. Although they had lost their low profile, Jesse and Frank James had gained the chance to become folk heroes.

The Civil War had devastated Clay County, Missouri, and the surrounding region, leaving many white citizens deeply unhappy. Southerners resented the power the Radical Republicans had gained and the rights that blacks now enjoyed. While Southern farmers were struggling just to survive, they watched corrupt politicians and rich Northern businessmen grow more prosperous. Wealthy eastern banks and railroads were particularly hated: the banks took away land from poor farmers when they fell behind on mortgage payments, and railroads cheaply acquired huge tracts of prime farmland from the government. Adding insult to injury, while the government raised taxes to finance railway bonds, the railroads charged farmers high shipping rates.

Consequently, Jesse James, the former Confederate soldier, drew cheers from the average farmer when he struck back at these powerful businesses. Newspaperman John Newman Edwards, one of Jesse's strongest allies, skillfully portrayed him as an honest everyman who was single-handedly waging war against the evil banks. (In his obituary of Jesse James, Edwards would lament, "Would to God he were alive today to make a righteous butchery of a few more of them.") While praising the James brothers' skill with guns and horses, Edwards asserted their innocence. Throughout their career, the journalist acted as a kind of public relations man, printing letters supposedly written by Jesse and writing editorials about the bandits' heroism.

Believing this noble image, many of Jesse's supporters spread largely fictional stories that depicted him as a kindhearted Robin Hood who stole from the rich to help the poor. One such tale recounted how Jesse and his gang once stopped to rest at a poor widow's small cabin on the way back from a holdup. Though she had little food, the widow gladly offered the men a meal. As she dished out the food, Jesse noticed tears running down her cheeks and asked why she was upset. The widow revealed that she had fallen behind on her mortgage payments and was about to lose her land. The banker was due that very day to foreclose on her farm unless she could come up with $800.

According to the legend, Jesse pulled $800 out of a sack and, over the woman's objections, insisted that she take it. After reminding her to get a receipt from the banker when she paid, he thanked the woman for her hospitality and left.

The banker arrived a few hours later, ready to force the widow off her land. When she handed him the money, the surprised man wrote a receipt and left. Three miles down the road, Jesse halted the banker at gunpoint and took back the cash. The widow kept her land, and Jesse had his money; only the "evil" bank lost.

Regardless of the truth of such tales, Jesse did cultivate a likable image. He was neat and clean-cut. A religious man, he neither swore nor

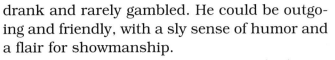

drank and rarely gambled. He could be outgoing and friendly, with a sly sense of humor and a flair for showmanship.

Jesse showed his mischievous side during his next robbery, which occurred in Corydon, Iowa, in June 1871. While Cole Younger and Clell Miller waited outside the town's bank, Jesse and Frank sauntered inside and pulled their usual routine of asking the cashier to make change for a $100 bill. When he asked why the bank and the streets were so empty, Jesse learned from the cashier that the townspeople were crowded into the church to listen to a popular politician.

After he tied up the cashier and robbed the bank, Jesse headed over to the meeting to have a little fun. He casually strolled in and interrupted the gathering, saying that there had been some trouble at the bank. While the crowd sat, stunned, Jesse began laughing loudly, strode out the door, and rode out of town with his amused gang.

In spite of the charm of these stories, the reality could be quite ugly. Underneath Jesse's lighthearted demeanor lurked a savage criminal who would do anything for money, even kill innocent people with little or no thought. Before one operation, a gang member asked him what would happen if someone in town sounded the alarm. Jesse responded chillingly, "We will shoot down anyone who interferes and if necessary clear the entire town out."

Jesse's disregard for other people was clear in one of his boldest robberies, which endangered scores of innocent men, women, and children. In 1872 he set his sights on the Kansas City Fair, an annual event that drew crowds of up to 10,000 each day and made its organizers a great deal of money. On September 26 Jesse, along with Cole and John Younger, rode through the throng of unsuspecting fair patrons to the main gate. There, in broad daylight, they grabbed a metal box containing the admission fees. When a worker struggled to get the box back, the robbers shot at him. With so many people around, it was miraculous that no one got killed. But a stray bullet tore into a little girl's leg as the robbers made their escape.

When Jesse later opened the box, expecting a generous bounty, he was disappointed to discover less than $1,000. Fortunately for the fair organizers, most of their cash had been transported to the bank only moments before the heist. In the next day's paper, Edwards expressed some pity for the wounded girl but praised the bandits for their bravery.

Confident of the support of the press and much of the public, the bandits soon grew even bolder—and greedier. Because even their successful bank robberies could be expected to net only a few thousand dollars, the gang looked for bigger game. And they found it in an untapped source: the railroads.

Newspaperman John Newman Edwards did much to promote the image of Jesse James as an honest, decent man who was waging war against corrupt banks and railroads.

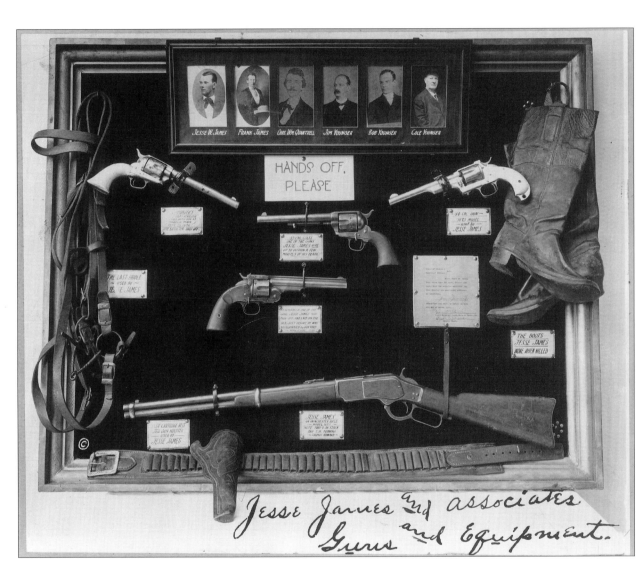

Jesse James and associates Guns and Equipment.

"Tell 'em to Come and Get Us"

After the Civil War, railroads expanded rapidly, crisscrossing the country and becoming an important means of transporting people and freight. To Jesse James, though, trains represented one thing: a ripe target for his gang. Impressive amounts of gold and cash traveled by rail from the West to the secure vaults of eastern banks. In addition, trains offered a captive group of passengers who possessed jewelry and other valuables. With the same amount of risk and effort, the gang could ride away from a train robbery carrying a much larger haul than they could get from a bank raid.

In July of 1873 the James-Younger gang learned that a Chicago, Rock Island, and Pacific Express train carrying more than $100,000—an incredible sum of money in those days—eastward would pass through Adair, Iowa, on the night of the 21st. Outside of town, the men scouted out an isolated section where the track

Tools of the trade: a display of guns and equipment Jesse James and his gang used.

curved around a bend. They loosened a rail, tied one end of a piece of rope around it, and replaced the rail so that the track appeared normal. Then they hid in nearby bushes and waited for the train to arrive.

Later that night, when the outlaws heard the train approaching, one of them yanked out the loosened rail. Engineer John Rafferty noticed the missing section at the last moment and, instead of thinking of his own safety and jumping free of the cabin, tried to slow the train by throwing the throttle into reverse. By then, however, the train had reached the missing segment and had started careening down the embankment. Rafferty was killed when the train's front car rolled over, but all of the passengers survived.

When the train skidded to a halt, the bandits jumped aboard, their faces hidden under white masks of the type worn by the Ku Klux Klan (a secret organization of white Southerners who terrorized blacks well into the 20th century). Instead of the expected bounty, Jesse found only a few thousand dollars in the safe—as a precaution, the gold had been sent on an earlier train. Angry at the small take, the gang stormed through the train, seizing jewelry and other possessions from the frightened passengers.

The dramatic train robbery made Jesse James a national figure. Even though the gang had simply robbed ordinary citizens, many people considered them heroes for attacking the railroads. But the powerful eastern businessmen who ran the railroads were infuriated. They quickly hired the Pinkerton National Detective Agency of Chicago to track down the bandits. Although the Pinkertons—as employees of the

agency were called—failed to catch the criminals after the Iowa incident, they were not about to give up the hunt. Allan Pinkerton, who had founded the agency in the 1850s, gained fame in 1861 when he uncovered a plot to assassinate Abraham Lincoln. During the Civil War, he gathered intelligence for the Union's Army of the Potomac and was head of counterespionage in Washington. He and his detectives had earned a reputation for cleverly and doggedly pursuing outlaws.

Meanwhile, the James gang continued its crime spree, ever more determined to grow rich and famous. With each new robbery, the bandits tried to spread their Robin Hood image. For instance, in January 1874 they robbed stage-

Allan Pinkerton (shown here during the Civil War) headed the Pinkerton National Detective Agency, which the railroads hired to bring the James gang to justice. When his agents bungled an attempt to capture Jesse and Frank James and instead killed their half-brother and wounded their mother, Pinkerton himself became a target. But after stalking the detective in Chicago, Jesse abandoned his quest for vengeance because he never got a chance to confront Pinkerton face to face.

An engraving showing the Gad's Hill train robbery of January 1874. By this time Jesse James had become infatuated with his Robin Hood image: during the robbery his men made a show of not taking anything from male passengers with calloused hands (who were presumably hardworking laborers).

coach passengers in Hot Springs, Arkansas, but loudly announced that they would take nothing from Confederate veterans. When one man, George Crump, declared that he had fought for the South, Cole Younger made a show of returning his watch and money.

Two weeks later the James gang pulled a similar stunt in Gad's Hill, Missouri, at the Iron Mountain Railroad station. After taking the signalmen hostage, Jesse placed a red flag on the tracks so the express train from St. Louis would stop. When the train pulled into the station, the gang members boarded with their guns drawn and proceeded to examine the palms of every male passenger. They explained that they would not steal from men with calloused hands, the sign of hardworking laborers.

Masters at creating a heroic image, the gang members acted as their own publicists. Before departing, Jesse handed a worker an envelope containing a written description of what had just occurred, with a blank space left for the railroad company to fill in the amount stolen (which turned out to be nearly $12,000). Jesse wanted this account of the robbery, which he labeled "the most daring on record," placed in newspapers. He added that because of the James gang's raid, there was "a hell of an excitement in this part of the country."

In fact, nearly the whole country found the outlaws' escapades exciting. The Robin Hood stories spread, causing some people to ignore the gang's ruthless acts of thievery and murder and to believe, instead, that the robbers were decent folks driven to crime by big business. Magazine stories and dime novels (melodramatic adventure tales that typically sold for 10 cents) painted Jesse James as a Wild West hero. Other robbers committed crimes using his name and style, and some people were even pleased to be robbed by the legendary outlaw. One stagecoach passenger told a reporter that "he was exceedingly glad, as he had to be robbed, that it was done by first class artists, by men of national reputation."

However, Jesse attracted some powerful enemies, and the Pinkertons continued their quest for his capture. In March 1874 agent John Whicher traveled to Jesse's hometown of Kearney, where he informed two prominent Clay County citizens that he planned to work as a laborer on the Samuel farm until the chance arose to arrest the James brothers. Despite being warned that the hot-tempered Zerelda Samuel and her boys were dangerous people and were highly suspicious of outsiders, Whicher set out for their farm.

Zerelda "Zee" Mimms, shown here in a school photo, was a cousin of Jesse's. In 1865 she nursed him back to health after he sustained a life-threatening chest wound, and the two fell in love. They were married in 1874.

Early the next morning, four men, including Jesse James, boarded a ferry and crossed the Missouri River to neighboring Jackson County. Smiling sinisterly, Jesse explained to the ferryman that the bound and gagged prisoner with them was a horse thief being taken to justice. The following morning, Whicher's body was found lying by the side of a road near the ferry with bullets in the head and chest.

Just a few days later, the Pinkerton agency was foiled again. Two Pinkertons and a deputy sheriff chased John and Jim Younger to southwestern Missouri and battled them in a vicious gunfight. Though John Younger was killed, Jim escaped after Pinkerton agent Louis J. Lull and deputy sheriff Edwin B. Daniel were mortally wounded. The three remaining Younger brothers continued to ride with the James gang.

In the middle of this trouble, Jesse enjoyed one of the happiest occasions of his life. On April 24, 1874, he married Zerelda Mimms in a ceremony officiated by his uncle, the Reverend William James, at a relative's home outside Kearney. He explained, "We had been engaged for nine years, and through good and evil report, and not withstanding the lies that have been told upon me and the crimes laid at my door, her devotion to me never wavered for a moment." He and his loyal Zee spent their honeymoon in Texas, where Jesse held up a few stagecoaches for fun.

When they returned to Missouri, the newlyweds found little peace because Jesse remained a hunted criminal. In January 1875 the Pinkerton agency made a third, even more disastrous attempt to apprehend him. In late 1874 agent Jack Ladd had hired on as a worker at Daniel Askew's farm, which bordered the Samuel homestead. Quietly blending in with the other Askew laborers, Ladd spied on the Samuel farm and waited until the James brothers came to visit their mother.

After Ladd sent word to the Pinkerton agency through a coded telegram, a special train arrived in Kearney on January 25, 1875, and unloaded a group of Pinkerton detectives. They cautiously surrounded the Samuel farm that night, keeping watch for the infamous brothers. In an attempt to force the cabin's inhabitants outside with smoke and fire, the agents tossed a device consisting of an iron ball surrounded by kerosene-soaked cotton through the kitchen window.

As the family rushed to investigate, a second missile flew through a window. Instead of simply producing smoke or setting the cabin on fire, as the agents had expected, one or both of the devices exploded after Dr. Samuel shoved them into the fireplace. Metal fragments shot around the room. One fragment killed nine-year-old Archie Samuel, Jesse's half-brother, and another badly injured his mother's right arm. Though Zerelda survived, her right hand had to be amputated.

The attempt to capture the James boys could not have gone worse for the Pinkertons. After the explosion, the agents panicked and fled the farm. In their haste, they left behind a revolver, which was marked with the initials "P. G. G." (for Pinkerton Government Guard, the name the agency used during the Civil War). This left no doubt as to who was behind the fiasco. The James brothers used their press connections to let the nation know what had happened and to create sympathy for their side of the story. Most newspapers around the country branded the Pinkertons cowards for the "savage and fiendish" act, and a grand jury indicted Allan Pinkerton and others for the murder of Archie Samuel.

Meanwhile, Jesse took his revenge. Jack Ladd disappeared the night of the explosion and was never seen again. Two months later an unidentified man gunned down Daniel Askew on his own front porch.

Jesse wanted one other man to pay for the raid—Allan Pinkerton. He traveled to Chicago and stalked the detective, but returned to Missouri unavenged. Jesse later revealed that he had passed up a handful of chances to murder Pinkerton, explaining, "I want him to know who did it. It wouldn't do me no good if I couldn't tell him about it before he died. I had a dozen chances to kill him when he didn't know it. I wanted to give him a fair chance but the opportunity never came."

His family's tragedy, however, did not discourage Jesse from his destructive life of crime. On July 7, 1876, the James gang stopped a Missouri Pacific train near Otterville, Missouri. The passengers were instructed to sing hymns while the bandits broke open the safe. As the thieves rode away $17,000 richer, Jesse yelled, "If you see any of the Pinkertons, tell 'em to come and get us."

Jesse did not realize how close authorities were to answering his taunts. After new gang member Hobbs Kerry boasted of his role in the Otterville holdup and flaunted large sums of money, the St. Louis police arrested him. Offered a lighter jail term in return for naming the other gang members, the shaken Kerry listed Jesse and Frank James, two of the Youngers, Clell Miller, Bill Chadwell, and Charlie Pitts. It was the first time that anyone involved with the gang had actually implicated Jesse James in a crime.

Jesse and his supporters reacted quickly in an attempt to control the damage. Zerelda Samuel vigorously defended her sons in public. And a letter supposedly written by Jesse that appeared in the *Kansas City Times* described Kerry's accusations as "a well-built pack of lies from beginning to end."

However, Kerry's confession, along with the dogged pursuit of Pinkerton's detectives, had weakened Jesse's position. A few short years earlier, Jesse had been widely viewed as a hero. Now people across the nation clamored for his arrest. Even citizens of Missouri, whom he had always been able to count on to shield him from the law, wondered if the time had come to bring him to justice. Many honest Missourians had worked hard to attract business to the area, and their efforts were constantly being undermined by the James gang's criminal deeds. Missouri's inability to capture such well-known outlaws made the state appear unsafe and its officials foolish and led to the nickname "the Bandit State."

Though Jesse James still had many supporters, his popularity had clearly begun to fade. In a short time, his image would be further tarnished—and his gang would be decimated—when a small Minnesota town turned the tables on the notorious outlaw.

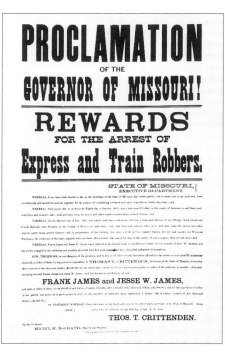

In this proclamation, issued on July 28, 1881, Missouri governor Thomas Crittenden offered a $5,000 reward for the arrest and conviction of any James gang member and $10,000 for the arrest and conviction of Jesse or Frank James. Among the crimes listed are the 1869 murder of bank cashier John Sheets and the murder of two railroad employees.

August Suborn, Swede Boy

Haywood, Cashr.

Glispin, Sheriff

Chadwell. Miller

Cole. Younger

Bob. Younger

Jim Younger

Charly. Pitts

Jacoby Photo

"Get Your Guns, Boys! They're Robbing the Bank"

The most-wanted man in Missouri, Jesse James decided it would be safer to commit his next crime outside the borders of his home state. When outlaw Bill Chadwell, a native Minnesotan, described the North Star State as a land full of banks ripe for the picking, Jesse's interest was piqued. Using Chadwell (also known as William Stiles) as their guide, the James brothers—along with Cole, Jim, and Bob Younger, Clell Miller, and Charlie Pitts (who also used the name Samuel Wells)—set out for

September 7, 1876, proved a fateful day for the people in this photo montage. Joseph Heywood, a cashier at the First National Bank of Northfield, Minnesota, was murdered for refusing to cooperate in an attempted James gang robbery. Northfield residents, including August Suborn, rallied to defend their town, killing outlaws Bill Chadwell and Clell Miller in the street. Charlie Pitts and the Younger brothers were wounded but managed to escape Northfield with their lives; Pitts was later killed and the Youngers were captured after a shoot-out with Sheriff James Glispin's posse.

southern Minnesota in August 1876.

The eight cutthroats traveled in a slow and orderly fashion to avoid attracting attention. The long linen dusters they wore over their clothes concealed their guns. Avoiding large cities, they posed as land dealers and cattle traders at each stop. As they headed north, Jesse and Frank scouted the countryside for escape routes and good hiding places.

The gang had intended to rob the bank in Mankato. But a man from Missouri recognized Jesse on the street and said hello as the outlaw was sizing up his target. Jesse quickly replied, "Hell, man, I don't know you," but the damage had already been done. The chance meeting, as well as the crowd that had gathered on the street, frightened the James gang away and spared Mankato.

The gang then rode 60 miles northeast to the town of Northfield. About 40 miles south of St. Paul on the eastern bank of the Cannon River, Northfield had a population of approximately 2,000, most of whom were farmers of Scandinavian origin. The town boasted two colleges, Carleton and St. Olaf, and was home to many thriving businesses. But Jesse's interest lay in the First National Bank, into which Northfield's farmers had recently deposited their profits from the wheat harvest.

On September 7, 1876, the gang entered Northfield in groups of twos and threes. Jesse James, Bob Younger, and Charlie Pitts rode in first and casually checked the street in front of the bank for potential trouble spots. The three then dismounted and entered J. G. Jeft's restaurant, where they ate ham and eggs while chatting with the owner and other customers. Jesse even offered to bet the owner $100 that the

Democrats would win the next state election.

Shortly after lunch the three outlaws were ready to make their move. They rode over to the bank, tied their horses out front, and went inside while Clell Miller and Cole Younger stood guard outside and Frank James, Jim Younger, and Bill Chadwell waited on the outskirts of town.

However, the gang members' actions did not go unnoticed. Across the street from the bank, Henry Wheeler, a medical student home on break from the University of Michigan, sat under the awning of his father's drugstore and carefully studied the movements of the unfamiliar men. Something about the strangers warned him to be on his guard.

The rest of the town realized that trouble was brewing when, as hardware store owner J. S. Allen tried to enter the bank, Clell Miller roughly grabbed him and told him to stay away.

A view of Northfield, Minnesota, circa 1870. Frank James, Jim Younger, and Bill Chadwell stood guard on the town's outskirts while the other men rode over the bridge and into the town square. The First National Bank, the gang's intended target, is the building with the arches to the right of center.

The interior of the First National Bank. Cashier Joseph Heywood attempted to lock Charlie Pitts in the vault at right.

Without a moment's hesitation, Allen broke free and ran around the corner, yelling, "Get your guns, boys! They're robbing the bank!"

Unlike the gang's other victims, the Northfield townspeople immediately rallied to defend themselves. As word of the robbery spread, men rushed for their weapons. Wheeler, the medical student, sped into the Hotel Dampier, where he found a gun and began shooting from a second-floor window. Businessman A. B. Manning also started firing from his lookout across the street.

Meanwhile, the three robbers inside the bank were also meeting resistance. Even after the criminals climbed over the wooden counter to reach the vault, cashier Joseph Heywood and clerk A. E. Bunker refused to hand over any money. When Pitts stepped into the open vault that housed the safe, Heywood boldly tried to shut the door to trap Pitts inside but was dragged away by the other two outlaws.

The bandits held a knife to Heywood's throat and commanded him to open the safe. Bravely ignoring the gang's threats, Heywood replied that the safe could not be opened because it had a time lock (a lock controlled by clockwork that could be opened only after a set time). This was just a clever bluff—although there was a time lock, the safe door was merely closed, not locked. Even though the bandits beat him and fired a shot to scare him, the stubborn cashier refused to cooperate.

Bunker, the clerk, also resisted courageously. When the frustrated robbers demanded to see the cash drawers, the clerk pointed to a small box that contained only a little money; he did not reveal the drawer under the counter where $3,000 was hidden. Even after Younger put his revolver to Bunker's temple, the clerk remained silent.

While the robbers ransacked the bank, unaware that the safe needed only a tug to open, Bunker rose from the floor and dashed toward the rear exit. Pitts shot him through the shoulder, but Bunker kept running out the door and into the alley. The clerk staggered into the street, screaming for help.

The three outlaws inside the bank finally became aware of the debacle that was taking place on the street when a gang member outside the bank yelled, "Better get out, boys. They're killing our men." Grabbing what little money they could, the robbers made for the door. Before leaving, Jesse walked over to Heywood, who was lying helplessly on the floor, and shot him in the head.

When they emerged from the bank, the bandits found themselves in a veritable shooting gallery. Bullets flew in all directions. Some townspeople had even begun to throw stones at the outlaws. Hearing the commotion, Frank James, Jim Younger, and Bill Chadwell had ridden in from their position on the edge of town to join the gunfight.

One of the first victims of the shoot-out was Nicholas Gustavson, a newly arrived Swede who spoke little English and did not understand the bandits when they told him to move out of the street. Northfield resident Elias Stacy registered the first hit on the outlaws. In all the excitement, however, he had mistakenly loaded his gun with bird shot, so while his blast at Clell Miller peppered Miller's face and knocked him off his horse, it did not seriously injure him. Miller climbed back on his horse and charged Stacy, who narrowly escaped death when the sharp-eyed Wheeler dropped Miller with one shot. Cole Younger rode up and shouted to Miller, but seeing that his companion was dead, he took Miller's guns and ammunition and hurried off.

Across the street from the bank, businessman Manning calmly ignored the bullets that were whizzing by his head while he searched for targets. His first shot felled Bob Younger's horse, and his next hit Cole Younger in the shoulder. He then spotted Chadwell, who was riding down the street, and, according to an eyewitness, aimed "as cool as though he was picking off a squirrel." Manning's shot pierced Chadwell through the heart, killing him instantly.

Incredibly, the sleepy town of Northfield was tearing apart the notorious James gang. As the shoot-out continued, Wheeler knocked off Cole Younger's hat with a shot, and another citizen hit Frank James in the leg. Jim Younger and Charlie Pitts also were wounded. Bob Younger sought shelter behind a stack of boxes, where he traded shots with Manning, who was on the other side of the street. Wheeler, who had a clearer view of Bob Younger from his second-story window, shattered the outlaw's right elbow with another accurate shot.

Realizing they were defeated, the remaining gang members beat a retreat toward the river as the townspeople kept up their deadly gunfire. Cole Younger, seeing that his brother Bob was injured and left without a horse, braved a hail of bullets to ride back and lift him onto his mount. The dazed brothers sped across the Cannon River Bridge to catch up with the other bandits.

In 20 furious minutes, the residents of Northfield had repelled the brutal gang that had terrified the nation. Determined to finally bring Jesse James and his cohorts to justice, the townspeople rushed to halt the outlaws' escape. The town's telegraph operator alerted the rest of the state, and posses from all over set out in hot pursuit of the criminals. The state of Minnesota quickly offered a $4,000 reward for their capture; the First National Bank added $700, and a railroad company threw in $500 per gang member.

By this time the gang was in a shambles. With Bill Chadwell dead, the outlaws had no one to guide them through the unfamiliar territory and were forced to head south blindly. And with Cole and Bob Younger riding two to a horse, the group could not move at top speed. After riding as fast as they could for a few miles, they had to stop to bandage their wounds. Jim and Cole Younger each had suffered painful injuries, and Bob Younger could do little with his shattered right elbow. Charlie Pitts bled from various wounds, and Frank James hobbled on a bad leg. Only Jesse had escaped with minor scratches.

Resting during the day and traveling slowly at night, the outlaws managed to evade the pos-

Sheriff James Glispin (far left) with the posse that captured the Younger brothers and killed Charlie Pitts near Madelia, Minnesota.

ses for four days. But for the first time in their nearly decade-long crime spree, the gang had no sympathetic farmers to turn to for help. They were forced to steal fresh horses when they could and sometimes traveled on foot, but their progress was slow.

When Bob Younger became too weak to ride a horse alone, Jesse proposed to either leave him behind or kill him. The other Youngers refused to abandon their brother, so the gang split up. Jesse and Frank headed west toward South Dakota, throwing the posses off their trail. The Younger brothers and Charlie Pitts continued to struggle along the southerly path.

One week after parting company with the James brothers, the four outlaws stopped at a farm near Madelia, Minnesota, 150 miles southwest of Northfield. When one of the gang approached a farmer to buy bread and eggs, the farmer's teenage son, Oscar Sorbel, noticed how awkwardly the stranger walked and saw an odd bulge under his coat. On a hunch, he rode into town to tell Sheriff James Glispin about the suspicious characters he had seen.

The sheriff immediately raised a posse and headed toward the farm. The bandits had little hope—they were outnumbered, and the posse knew the region's back roads far better. But they refused to surrender, and in the shoot-out that ensued, the posse raked them with bullets, killing Charlie Pitts and severely injuring the Youngers. Finally Bob Younger, the only one left standing, surrendered.

The infamous bandits were taken into custody and treated for their injuries. Cole Younger had received at least seven additional wounds in the gunfight with the posse, including one from a rifle ball lodged under his right eye. Jim Younger had been hit five times, while his brother Bob was still pained by the injuries he sustained in Northfield. All three survived, however, and were sentenced to 25-year prison terms in Minnesota. Bob Younger died of tuberculosis in prison in 1889; his brother Jim shot himself in 1902 after being paroled. Only Cole—who walked around with 11 bullets still in his body—enjoyed freedom again. He was paroled in 1901, received an official pardon in 1903, and lived quietly until his death in Missouri in 1916.

Jesse and Frank James fared far better. Without the more severely wounded gang members to slow them down, the pair soon crossed into the Dakota Territory. By September 17, just 10 days after the disastrous Northfield robbery, they were headed toward Sioux City, Iowa. There they forced a local physician, Dr. Mosher, to switch clothes and horses with them. Eluding posses in four states, Jesse and Frank returned to Missouri, where they could breathe easier. Though Jesse escaped Northfield with his life, his gang would never again be the same.

"Never Known a Day of Perfect Peace"

Although Jesse had miraculously recovered from serious wounds and made amazing escapes in the past, his luck now seemed to be running out. The Northfield raid had enraged the nation, and more detectives than ever were searching for the infamous brothers, making even Clay County unsafe. Jesse and Frank were forced to remain out of sight for three long years.

The brothers settled near Nashville, Tennessee. There they traded their outlaw ways for lives of honest workingmen and turned their attention to raising their families. Frank, who had taken the alias B. J. Woodson, and his wife, Annie, became parents to Robert Franklin on February 6, 1878. Jesse, who used the name J. D. Howard, had first become a father on December 31, 1875, when Jesse Edwards (named in honor of loyal newspaperman John Newman Edwards) was born. Shortly after the family arrived in Tennessee, Zee (who used the name Josie Howard) gave birth to twins who

Jesse James, dead at the age of 34.

died days later, but on July 17, 1879, the couple was blessed with a healthy girl they named Mary.

The Woodsons and the Howards appeared to be typical families and blended into the community. Both men became farmers, with Frank also working at a lumber company and Jesse working as a wheat merchant. The tall, blue-eyed, bearded J. D. Howard attended a Methodist church regularly, and the men's only apparent vice was horse racing. Both voted in local elections and seemed to be law-abiding citizens.

While Frank readily settled into the calm life of farming, Jesse grew restless and, in 1879, ventured west to explore the possibility of ranching. He stayed in Las Vegas, New Mexico, at a hotel run by his old friend W. Scott Moore. There, according to one legend, Moore introduced him to another infamous hotel guest: William Bonney, better known as Billy the Kid. Supposedly the two outlaws compared notes and talked of joining forces. But in the end, Jesse decided that a partnership with Billy would be a bad idea and that starting a ranch would require too much money. He headed home, still searching for a more exciting alternative to farming.

In late 1879 Jesse decided to return to his criminal ways and formed a new gang. Frank refused to take part, but Jesse rounded up Ed Miller, Wood Hite, Bill Ryan, Dick Liddil, and Tucker Bassham. This new group differed from Jesse's other gangs in one critical respect: Unlike his earlier riders—many of whom had been killed or jailed—these men had not been Jesse's brothers-in-arms during the Civil War. Greed, rather than loyalty, was this gang's primary bond.

Jesse hurtled back into the national spotlight on October 8, 1879, when he and his five recruits robbed the Chicago and Alton Railroad near Glendale, Missouri. After seizing $6,000 from the safe, Jesse supposedly walked up to the engineer and said, "I didn't get your name, but mine is Jesse James." A month later the newspapers' front pages carried more sensational headlines: former gang member George Shepherd claimed to have killed the notorious outlaw.

Allan Pinkerton's son Robert, himself a detective who had spent years on the trail of Jesse James, scoffed at Shepherd's tall tale and vowed to continue his chase. He explained, "I consider Jesse James the worst man, without exception, in America. He is utterly devoid of fear."

Newspapers seconded Pinkerton's opinion, condemning the James gang for frightening people away from Missouri. For instance, the *New York Illustrated News* declared, "When a traveler got into a Missouri train he did so with the same feeling that a man has when going into battle—with little expectation of getting through alive." No longer blinded by the Robin Hood legends, the country was finally recognizing Jesse James for what he was—a ruthless criminal.

Even in Jesse's home state, people's views of the outlaw had changed. Democrat Thomas Crittenden ran for governor in 1880 on the promise to rid Missouri of the James gang—either by their arrest or by their death. Voters, weary of Jesse's criminal exploits, elected Crittenden, who served notice on the bandit in his first speech as governor: "We should let all know that Missouri cannot be the home and abiding place of lawlessness of any character." William H. Wallace, the newly elected prosecutor in Jackson County, also denounced Jesse

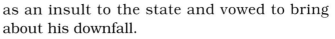

as an insult to the state and vowed to bring about his downfall.

The prosecutor's first official action in this regard came in March 1881, after one of Jesse's gang, Bill Ryan, got drunk and foolishly boasted that he was a feared outlaw. In addition to the Glendale train heist, Ryan had been involved in the September 1880 robbery of a tourist stagecoach near Mammoth Cave, Kentucky. He may also have known about Jesse's holdup of a government paymaster in Muscle Shoals, Alabama, in early 1881. Despite death threats, Wallace brought Ryan to trial for the Glendale crime.

Disregarding the changing tide of public opinion, Jesse persisted in his life of crime. As soon as Ryan was arrested, Jesse and his family cleared out of Nashville. After spending some time in Kentucky, he boldly returned to Kansas City, confident that he would not be captured. While lawmen still had no accurate physical description of him, Jesse knew his pursuers by sight and often taunted them by sending notes describing where and when he had spotted them on his trail. Always cocky, Jesse felt secure that his Clay County friends and neighbors would support and protect him.

However, the outlaw's barbaric behavior in his next crime destroyed the last vestiges of his public support. On July 15, 1881, the James brothers (Frank had returned to the gang a few months earlier for the Muscle Shoals heist), their cousins Wood and Clarence Hite, and Dick Liddil boarded a Rock Island train headed east from Kansas City. While they waited in their seats, pretending to be regular passengers, Jesse recognized the conductor, William Westfall, as the man who had run the Pinkertons' train the night his half-brother was killed and his mother's arm injured. Without a word, Jesse fatally shot Westfall in the back. As the passengers around them screamed, Frank James killed a man named Frank McMillan for no apparent reason. A third person was brutally beaten before the five outlaws grabbed $10,000 and disappeared into the night.

An outraged Governor Crittenden swore that he would bring the criminals to justice. After meeting with representatives of the railroad companies, Crittenden announced that a fantastic $55,000 in reward money was being posted for the arrest of the James gang. Jesse and Frank were each worth $10,000, dead or alive. Crittenden hoped that the money would entice a James gang member into surrendering and delivering the leaders to the authorities.

Undeterred, Jesse continued to attack the railroads. On September 7, 1881—exactly five years after the Northfield catastrophe—he led Frank, Dick Liddil, Clarence and Wood Hite, and Charlie Ford to Blue Cut Ravine, near Glendale, Missouri. There they stopped a train that was supposed to be carrying $100,000. When Jesse discovered that they had attacked the wrong train and that the safe held only a few thousand dollars, he beat a train worker senseless with the butt of his gun. The gang then robbed the passengers, announcing that it was an act of revenge for the railroads' reward offer.

After this incident, Governor Crittenden and Jackson County prosecutor William Wallace redoubled their efforts to destroy the gang. Wallace convinced a James gang member, Tucker Bassham, to testify against Bill Ryan in exchange for a pardon from the governor. Bassham had to flee the state after a mob of old

Mary and Jesse Edwards, the children of Jesse and Zee James.

Confederates torched his home, but his testimony did its damage. Bill Ryan was sentenced to 25 years in prison, the first time that a jury from one of Jesse's strongholds had convicted a James gang member.

Unable to withstand the pressure, the gang began to fall apart at the seams. Jesse soon became suspicious of his fellow outlaws. When Ed Miller mentioned that he was thinking about giving up crime, Jesse took him out for a ride. New gang member Charlie Ford remembered that Jesse returned alone and "said Miller was in bad health, and he did not think he could live long." Shortly afterward, Miller's body, with a gunshot wound to the head, was discovered lying by the side of a country road. Gang member Jim Cummings fled the state to avoid a similar fate.

Sensing that he was unsafe, Jesse moved his family to St. Joseph, Missouri, about 60 miles west of Kansas City, in November 1881. Under the name Thomas Howard, he settled into his so-called House on the Hill, which allowed him to see who was approaching on all sides. "He was so watchful," Charlie Ford said, "no man could get the drop on him." Jesse kept two horses, one always saddled and bridled, and, according to legend, even slept with pistols in his hands.

But no matter how watchful he was, Jesse could not control the actions of his gang members. In December, Dick Liddil, Wood Hite, and Bob and Charlie Ford gathered at the house of Martha Bolton, the Fords' widowed sister. After Liddil and Hite got into an argument over the division of the loot from the Blue Cut robbery and began shooting at each other, Bob Ford drew his revolver and killed Hite. Knowing that

Jesse would seek revenge when he learned of his cousin's death, Bob and Charlie Ford decided to betray him for the reward money.

The Fords sent their sister Martha to meet with William Wallace and Governor Crittenden. She relayed the message that the Fords would hand over Jesse in return for the reward money and freedom for Dick Liddil, who would surrender to authorities and testify against other gang members. On January 13, 1882, Crittenden and Bob Ford held a secret meeting and hammered out their deal. Both agreed that Jesse was not to be taken alive. Eleven days later, Liddil surrendered and began telling all he knew about the James gang; his information led to the arrest of Jesse's other cousin, Clarence Hite, who pleaded guilty to train robbery.

Nearly everyone Jesse had trusted was now imprisoned or dead. Still unaware of their plot, Jesse asked his remaining gang members, Charlie and Bob Ford, to move in with him while they plotted their next crime. On March 31 Bob Ford visited the Clay County sheriff, informing him that Jesse had handed them a golden opportunity and they just had to wait for the right moment to seize it.

They would not wait long. Living with Jesse and his family while planning his murder was making the Fords extremely nervous. Around the first of April, Jesse read a newspaper article detailing Dick Liddil's confession, which had implicated both James brothers. Charlie Ford—who Jesse knew had been close to Liddil—worried that Jesse would kill him as soon as they completed their upcoming robbery. And the scowl that covered Jesse's face so rattled Bob Ford that he later recalled, "I knew then I had placed my head in the lion's mouth. How could

From the cover of a dime novel: Bob Ford brings the outlaw career of Jesse James to an end.

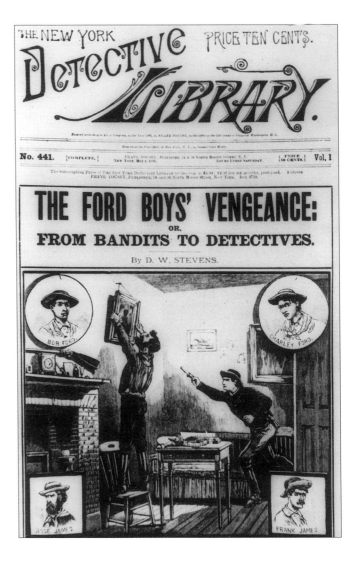

I safely remove it?" They had to do the deed as soon as possible, he believed, or they would both end up dead.

On April 3, 1882, the Fords saw their chance. While Zee worked in the kitchen and the two James children played in the yard after breakfast, Jesse moved to dust and straighten a picture on the wall. Strangely, he took off his revolvers first, laying them on the bed. Possibly he feared being seen through the window, or perhaps he wanted to trick the Fords into believing that he still trusted them so that he could catch them off guard later. At any rate, after removing his guns, he climbed onto a chair to reach the top of the picture and turned his back to the brothers. Bob Ford silently drew his revolver but made a slight noise as he cocked the hammer. As Jesse turned, Bob Ford shot him in the back of the head.

Jesse collapsed onto the floor, and the Ford brothers dashed out of the house. Zee rushed into the room and cradled her husband's bloody head in her arms, where he died moments later. He was 34 years old. When lawmen arrived to investigate, Zee revealed Jesse's true identity and sobbed, "A kinder-hearted and truer man to his family never lived."

As news of the murder spread, great crowds gathered to view the body and take souvenirs from the crime scene. Zerelda Samuel arrived the next day and made a fierce impression at the coroner's inquest. Glaring at Dick Liddil, she yelled, "Look at me, you traitor. Look upon me, the broken mother, and on this poor wife and her children. . . . With the coward you are, God will have vengeance!" She and Zee took Jesse's body back to Kearney, where he was laid to rest on the Samuel farm at a funeral attended by hundreds.

Although he longed to attend the funeral and comfort his mother, Frank James, who was living in Baltimore, feared he would be arrested if he returned to Missouri. In the months after the shooting, his wife and John Newman Edwards, the newspaperman, talked with Governor Crittenden, who guaranteed that Frank would receive a fair trial if he turned himself in. On

October 5, 1882, Edwards accompanied Frank to the governor's office. As he passed Crittenden his revolvers, the outlaw said, "I want to hand over to you that which no living man except myself has been permitted to touch since 1861, and to say that I am your prisoner."

Frank's action created a sensation. Everyone was eager to finally catch a glimpse of the infamous bandit. When asked by a reporter why he surrendered, Frank painted a vivid picture of the unglamorous realities of criminal life:

> I was tired of an outlaw's life. I have been hunted for twenty-one years. I have literally lived in the saddle. I have never known a day of perfect peace. It was one long, anxious, inexorable, eternal vigil. When I slept it was literally in the midst of an arsenal. If I heard dogs bark more fiercely than usual, or the feet of horses in a greater volume of sound than usual, I stood to my arms. Have you any idea of what a man must endure who leads such a life? No, you cannot. No one can unless he lives it for himself.

After more than 15 years of thievery and murder, Frank James finally stood trial on a number of charges. The court case was a public spectacle that attracted more attention, the newspapers claimed, than the trial of President James Garfield's assassin. Prosecutor William Wallace argued eloquently and called nearly 90 witnesses to prove Frank's guilt, but the celebrated outlaw had eight skilled attorneys and other powerful allies on his side. Thirty-nine witnesses testified on his behalf, including Joseph Shelby, the popular former Confederate general. The jury acquitted Frank on all charges. After a second trial in which he was also acquitted, Frank spent the remainder of his life quietly, farming and performing other jobs until his death on February 18, 1915.

As for Bob and Charlie Ford, they never found peace after the killing of Jesse James. They thought they had achieved a remarkable feat, declaring, "We feel proud we have killed an outlaw known over the whole world." But it was Jesse James, the notorious outlaw, who—now that he was gone—received the public's sympathy. Many people saw the Fords as traitors who had destroyed a legend. When they stood trial for the murders of Jesse James and Wood Hite, the brothers had to be protected from angry mobs. After being sentenced to hang, they were pardoned by the governor and quietly given the reward money.

Always afraid of being killed by one of Jesse's relatives, Charlie Ford finally shot himself in the head several years later. Bob Ford, who made a living reenacting the infamous shooting in Wild West shows as well as in P. T. Barnum's circus, became an object of scorn. A popular song referred to him as "that dirty little coward that shot Mr. Howard." In 1892 he was gunned down by Ed Kelly, who wanted to be remembered as "the man who shot the man who shot Jesse James."

Jesse's legend continued to grow in the years after his death. Some people refused to believe that he had been killed, insisting that his death was a hoax, just as George Shepherd's earlier claim had been. For years afterward, impersonators claiming to be the outlaw popped up. The public's appetite for information about him seemed endless—tourists flocked to the Samuel farm and the House on the Hill just to glimpse where he had lived and died. Frank James and

Frank James, photographed in 1898 at age 55. After the death of his brother, Frank surrendered to authorities and was twice tried and acquitted. He lived quietly until his death in 1915.

Cole Younger became popular attractions in a traveling Wild West show. And even Jesse James, Jr., got into the act, appearing in a silent movie called *Under the Black Flag* as a publicity stunt.

Jesse James continues to fascinate people today. Countless books and movies have explored his colorful life and the role he played in the Wild West's history. Every September, Northfield residents reenact the fateful raid at their yearly festival. Jesse even captured headlines as recently as July 1995, when a court allowed scientists to exhume, or dig up, his remains and perform genetic tests in an attempt to disprove claims that he staged his own death and actually lived into the 20th century. (The tests indicated that the remains were, indeed, those of the outlaw.) Jesse James—fearless Confederate guerrilla, false Robin Hood, and ruthless thief and murderer—remains a legend of the American West.

THE JAMES GANG'S ROBBERIES

CHRONOLOGY

1847   Jesse Woodson James is born to Robert and Zerelda James on September 5 in Kearney, Missouri

1850   Robert James dies of pneumonia in California

1855   Zerelda marries her third husband, Dr. Reuben Samuel

1864   Sixteen-year-old Jesse joins his older brother, Frank, in a Confederate guerrilla unit, where he perfects his riding and shooting techniques; he survives a serious chest wound

1865   While trying to surrender, Jesse is shot by Federal soldiers, sustaining a second severe chest wound; his first cousin Zerelda "Zee" Mimms nurses him back to health; Jesse and Zee become engaged

1867   Jesse James participates in a failed bank robbery in Savannah, Missouri; the James-Younger gang successfully steals $4,000 from the Hughes and Mason Bank in Richmond, Missouri, killing three townspeople

1869   Jesse James murders cashier and former Union army captain John W. Sheets on December 7 during a bank robbery in Gallatin, Missouri

1872   Jesse and Cole and John Younger rob the Kansas City Fair on September 26

1873   Jesse James and his gang pull their first train heist on July 21 in Adair, Iowa

1874   John Whicher, a detective from the Pinkerton agency, is found dead after setting out to capture Jesse James; John Younger is killed by Pinkertons; Jesse and Zee marry on April 24

1875   Pinkerton detectives throw smoke bombs into the Samuel house on January 25; they detonate after being tossed into a fireplace, killing Jesse's nine-year-old half-brother, Archie Samuel, and maiming his mother; Zee and Jesse's son, Jesse Edwards, is born on December 31

1876   Townspeople in Northfield, Minnesota, thwart an attempted bank robbery and decimate the James-Younger gang; Jesse and Frank James escape and settle in Nashville, Tennessee

1879   Jesse's second child, Mary, is born July 17; on October 8, he leads five new gang members in a $6,000 train robbery near Glendale, Missouri

1881   Jesse and Frank James and three gang members rob a train on July 15, killing two and escaping with $10,000; Missouri governor Thomas Crittenden responds by posting rewards of $10,000 each for Jesse and Frank James

1882   Gang member Bob Ford meets with Governor Crittenden on January 13 and agrees to kill Jesse James; Ford and his brother Charlie move in with the James family; on April 3, Bob Ford fatally shoots Jesse in the back of the head; Frank James surrenders to authorities on October 5

1995   Scientists get legal permission to exhume the body in Jesse James's grave; DNA tests indicate that the remains are indeed his, dispelling persistent rumors that he staged his own death in 1882

FURTHER READING

Breihan, Carl W. *The Complete and Authentic Life of Jesse James.* New York: Frederick Fell, 1953.

Castel, Albert. *"Men Behind the Masks: The James Brothers." American History Illustrated* 17 (June 1982): 1018.

Catton, Bruce. *The American Heritage Picture History of the Civil War.* New York: American Heritage Publishing, 1960.

Croy, Homer. *Jesse James Was My Neighbor.* New York: Duell, Sloan and Pearce, 1949.

Ernst, John. *Jesse James.* Englewood Cliffs, N.J.: Prentice-Hall, 1976.

Green, Carl R., and William R. Sanford. *Jesse James.* Hillside, N.J.: Enslow Publishers, 1992.

Horan, James D. *Desperate Men.* New York: Doubleday, 1962.

_____. *The Authentic Wild West: The Outlaws.* New York: Crown, 1977.

Nash, Jay Robert. *Bloodletters and Bad Men.* New York: Evans Press, 1973.

Stiles, T. J. *Jesse James.* New York: Chelsea House Publishers, 1994.

Trachtman, Paul. *The Old West: The Gunfighters.* New York: Time-Life Books, 1974.

Triplett, Frank. *The Life, Times and Treacherous Death of Jesse James.* Chicago: The Swallow Press, 1970.

Wellman, Paul I. *A Dynasty of Western Outlaws.* New York: Doubleday, 1977.

PICTURE CREDITS

Every effort has been made to contact the copyright owners of photographs and illustrations used in this book. In the event that the holder of a copyright has not heard from us, he or she should contact Chelsea House Publishers.

page 2 The Bettmann Archive
10 University of Oklahoma Library, Western History Collections
12 Library of Congress
15 Library of Congress
16 Jackson County Historical Society
19 State Historical Society of Missouri, Columbia
20 UPI/Bettmann Newsphotos
23 State Historical Society of Missouri, Columbia
24 State Historical Society of Missouri, Columbia
27 State Historical Society of Missouri, Columbia
28 Library of Congress
31 The Bettmann Archive
32 State Historical Society of Missouri, Columbia
34 Jackson County Historical Society
37 State Historical Society of Missouri, Columbia
38 Minnesota Historical Society
41 Minnesota Historical Society
42 Northfield Historical Society
46 Northfield Historical Society
48 The Bettmann Archive
53 Library of Congress
56 The Bettmann Archive
59 State Historical Society of Missouri, Columbia
61 Map Illustration, Gary Tong

INDEX

ABOUT THE AUTHOR

John F. Wukovits is a teacher and writer from Trenton, Michigan, who specializes in history and sports. His work has appeared in more than 25 national publications, including *Wild West* and *America's Civil War*. His books include a biography of the World War II commander Admiral Clifton Sprague and biographies of Barry Sanders and Vince Lombardi for Chelsea House. A graduate of the University of Notre Dame, Wukovits is the father of three daughters—Amy, Julie, and Karen.